Prayers for the Journey

Scripture Prayer Praise

VCNETTLES INSPIRATIONS AND LETTERS

Vernet Clemons Nettles, EdD

VCNettles Inspirations and Letters
Montgomery, AL

www.vernetcnettles.com
vernetcnettles@gmail.com

ISBN - 979-8-9892081-3-5

Acknowledgements

First and always giving honor to God...

Thank you so much to my grandparents, who watch over me from the peaceful blue skies of heaven. My grandmothers were prayer warriors and my grandfathers believed in the love of God.

Thank you to my parents who taught me the importance of church family, grace-ful relationships, and worship. Their words of wisdom and guidance come back to my mind and heart at the strangest moments which make me smile.

A special thank you to each of them for pouring into me, my siblings, and my siblings-in-love the power of love, prayer, and faith.

Dedication

This book is dedicated to Change...

the changes in life that always come whether we are ready or not.

Each section - ***Guidance, Strength, Comfort, and Praise*** - represents the connection we seek in our relationship with God as we journey through this life.

Change can be frightening, exhilarating, thoughtful, unexpected, life-altering and/or life-elevating. Yet, with each step of change, we must seek God in each moment. These prayers were written out of my heart's desire to embrace the changes in my life over these last few years. It is my hope that these prayers provide you with the comfort and connection that they did for me.

Thank you and as always.
Hugs

Table of Contents

Prayers for the Journey

The Call

The Call

"Come to Me, all you who labor and are heavy laden, and I will give you rest. Take My yoke upon you and learn from Me, for I am gentle and lowly in heart, and you will find rest for your souls."

Matthew 11:28-29 NKJV

Prayers for the Journey

Guidance

I. *Guidance*

"If any of you lacks wisdom, let him ask of God, who gives to all liberally and without reproach, and it will be given to him."

James 1:5 NKJV

Heavenly Father, I ask you today for wisdom. I am reminded that my wisdom is connected to my relationship with you. It is my opportunity to make decisions with you according to your will for my life. Please, Lord, guide me. In Jesus' name, we pray. **Amen.**

II. Guidance

"Be anxious for nothing, but in everything by prayer and supplication, with thanksgiving, let your requests be made known to God;"

Philippians 4:6 NKJV

Heavenly Father, thank you for your Word that reminds us to bring our worries to you. Thank you for reminders and gentle whispers that calm my spirit and soothe my soul. Thank you for reminding me to pray and not worry. In Jesus' name, we pray. **Amen.**

III. *Guidance*

"Look at the birds of the air, for they neither sow nor reap nor gather into barns; yet your heavenly Father feeds them. Are you not of more value than they?"

Matthew 6:26 NKJV

Glorious Father, thank you for your promises. Thank you for reminding me not to worry, because just as you feed the carefree birds, you will take care of me. Thank you for your outpouring of love and protection. In Jesus' name, we pray. **Amen.**

IV. *Guidance*

"Your hands have made me and fashioned me; Give me understanding, that I may learn Your commandments."

Psalm 119:73 NKJV

My Lord, thank you for a love that fashioned me according to your desires. Please give me understanding so that I may learn your Word and your purpose for my life. Pour into me your Spirit, so that others may see you. In Jesus' name, we pray. **Amen.**

V. Guidance

"Trust in the LORD with all your heart, And lean not on your own understanding;

Proverbs 3:5 NKJV

Heavenly Father, there are places and spaces in my life that I do not understand, and I struggle for purpose. Your Word says we should depend on you. I trust you, Lord, and believe that as I strive to walk with you, you will direct my path. In Jesus' name, we pray. **Amen.**

VI. *Guidance*

"A wise man will hear and increase learning, And a man of understanding will attain wise counsel,"

Proverbs 1:5 NKJV

Heavenly Father, I pray for wisdom in my life. I seek guidance and understanding that only you can bring. Show me I pray, the path for our lives. Open my ears so that I can hear; open my heart so that I may enjoy the sweet communion of the Holy Spirit. In Jesus' name, we pray. **Amen.**

VII. *Guidance*

"But the Helper, the Holy Spirit, whom the Father will send in My name, He will teach you all things, and bring to your remembrance all things that I said to you."

John 14:26 NKJV

Heavenly Father, Father, we are grateful for your Holy Spirit that guides us and teaches us your Word. We pray to let go of our worries and our fears. We also pray for your strength, so that we may release our will and embrace your will for us. In Jesus' name, we pray. **Amen.**

Prayers for the Journey

Strength

I *Strength*

"The Lord is my strength and my shield; My heart trusted in Him, and I am helped; Therefore my heart greatly rejoices, And with my song I will praise Him."

Psalm 28:7 NKJV

Glorious Father, thank you for being my strength and my shield. Thank you for your guidance and your love that causes my heart to leap for joy and be at peace because you go before me in the presence of my struggles. In Jesus' name, we pray. **Amen.**

II. Strength

"Have I not commanded you? Be strong and of good courage; do not be afraid, nor be dismayed, for the Lord your God is with you wherever you go."

Joshua 1:9 NKJV

Heavenly Father, thank you for your encouragement that reminds me to be strong and to let go of my fear and distress because you are with me. Thank you for being with me on my battlefields, and for your ever-present comfort. In Jesus' name, we pray. **Amen.**

III. *Strength*

"Fear not, for I am with you; Be not dismayed, for I am your God. I will strengthen you, Yes, I will help you, I will uphold you with My righteous right hand."

Isaiah 41:10 NKJV

My God of Comfort and of Peace, I struggle with the trials of the world around me and my soul grows weary. But your Word reminds me that you are my God, you are my help, and you are my strength. Thank you, Lord. In Jesus' name, we pray. **Amen.**

IV. *Strength*

"But those who wait on the Lord Shall renew their strength; They shall mount up with wings like eagles, They shall run and not be weary, They shall walk and not faint."

Isaiah 40:31 NKJV

Father God, thank you for reminding me to run on. You have promised to renew my strength. Thank you for reminding me that as I wait for you and remain faithful, you will put all things in order according to your will. In Jesus' name, we pray. **Amen.**

V. Strength

"For God has not given us a spirit of fear, but of power and of love and of a sound mind."

II Timothy 1:7 NKJV

My Lord, thank you for your Word that reminds me to put away my fears as your love is my courage to face what I feel is impossible. Grant me discernment and grace as I continue along this path. In Jesus' name, we pray. **Amen.**

IV. Strength

"But those who wait on the Lord Shall renew their strength; They shall mount up with wings like eagles, They shall run and not be weary, They shall walk and not faint."

Isaiah 40:31 NKJV

Father God, thank you for reminding me to run on. You have promised to renew my strength. Thank you for reminding me that as I wait for you and remain faithful, you will put all things in order according to your will. In Jesus' name, we pray. **Amen.**

VII. *Strength*

"Be strong and of good courage, do not fear nor be afraid of them; for the LORD your God, He is the One who goes with you. He will not leave you nor forsake you."

Deuteronomy 31:6 NKJV

Glorious Father, forgive me when I am anxious and fearful about the changes and the battles in my life. Thank you for your encouragement and assurance that you are always with me. In Jesus' name, we pray. **Amen.**

Prayers for the Journey

Comfort

I. *Comfort*

"Finally, brethren, whatever things are true, whatever things are noble, whatever things are just, whatever things are pure, whatever things are lovely, whatever things are of good report, if there is any virtue and if there is anything praiseworthy—meditate on these things."

Philippians 4:8 NKJV

My Lord, thank you for reminding me to meditate on all things true, noble, and pure. Thank you for reminding me to focus on each time you have delivered me and all things praiseworthy - your love, your grace, and your mercy. In Jesus' name, we pray. ***Amen.***

II. Comfort

"Blessed be the God and Father of our Lord Jesus Christ, the Father of mercies and God of all comfort, who comforts us in all our tribulation, that we may be able to comfort those who are in any trouble, with the comfort with which we ourselves are comforted by God."

II Corinthians 1:3-4 NKJV

Heavenly Father, thank you for your comfort in all situations - in good times and challenging times. Thank you for creating me with your love and strength, so that I can pour into others. In Jesus' name, we pray. **Amen.**

III. Comfort

"He makes me to lie down in green pastures; He leads me beside the still waters."

Psalm 23:2 NKJV

Heavenly Father, thank you for making me to lie down. Thank you for giving me an opportunity to rest and restore myself back to you. Thank you for the stillness so that I can hear you again and be reminded that you are God and all will be well. In Jesus' name, we pray. **Amen.**

IV. Comfort

"Come to Me, all you who labor and are heavy laden, and I will give you rest."

Matthew 11:28 NKJV

My Lord, I come to you tired - tired of feeling helpless; tired of situations that I cannot control; tired of feeling unfulfilled; and tired of being tired. I am here to exchange my burdens for your grace, and I am grateful. In Jesus' name, we pray. **Amen.**

V. *Comfort*

"Then they cried out to the LORD in their trouble, And He saved them out of their distresses. He sent His word and healed them, And delivered them from their destructions."

Psalm 107:19-20 NKJV

God of Deliverance, your Word brings me healing and deliverance. Father, as I focus on you and your presence in my life, I am reminded that through you I can conquer anything. Please bring me closer to you. In Jesus' name, we pray. **Amen.**

VI. Comfort

"Likewise the Spirit also helps in our weaknesses. For we do not know what we should pray for as we ought, but the Spirit Himself makes intercession for us with groanings which cannot be uttered."

Romans 8:26 NKJV

Father of Comfort, thank you for knowing my deepest cries that I cannot find words to speak. Thank you for interceding on my behalf for standing in my gap and for filling me when I am empty. In Jesus' name, we pray. **Amen.**

VII. Comfort

"Have You not made a hedge around him, around his household, and around all that he has on every side? You have blessed the work of his hands, and his possessions have increased in the land."

Job 1:10 NKJV

Gracious Lord, thank you for placing your arms of protection around me. I have many challenges and I can become anxious. But I am comforted when I realize that you have promised to protect me. Thank you for blessing me, my family, and the work you have charged me to do. In Jesus' name, we pray. **Amen.**

Prayers for the Journey

Praise

I. Praise

"The Lord has appeared of old to me, saying: "Yes, I have loved you with an everlasting love; Therefore with lovingkindness I have drawn you."

Jeremiah 31:3 NKJV

Heavenly Father, thank you for your loving kindness that is ever and always present. You have always beckoned me close to you, and I am grateful for your promises that cover me now and throughout my life. In Jesus' name, we pray. **Amen.**

II. Praise

"I will praise You, for I am fearfully and wonderfully made; Marvelous are Your works, And that my soul knows very well."

Psalm 139:14 NKJV

Glorious Father, thank you for making me and seeing me as marvelous. Help me to see myself in your eyes - fearfully and wonderfully made. Father, you are marvelous, and great are your blessings. In Jesus' name, we pray. **Amen**.

III. Praise

"And in that day you will say: "Praise the Lord, call upon His name; Declare His deeds among the peoples, Make mention that His name is exalted."

Isaiah 12:4 NKJV

My God, My Father, thank you for all that you have done. As I remember the challenges and the triumphs, I praise you because you have delivered me each and every time. Thank you for being great and greatly to be praised. In Jesus' name, we pray. **Amen.**

IV. Praise

"But at midnight Paul and Silas were praying and singing hymns to God, and the prisoners were listening to them."

Acts 16:25 NKJV

Father God, thank you for reminding me that even in my darkest hour to praise your holy name. Father, I glorify you and magnify your name. Father, give me a praise that others may also hear. In Jesus' name, we pray. **Amen.**

V. Praise

"Sing to the Lord, bless His name; Proclaim the good news of His salvation from day to day."

Psalm 96:2 NKJV

Father God, I bless your name and shout Glory Hallelujah, for you are great and greatly to be praised. I sing my song of thanksgiving as I glory in all of your blessings. Thank you for your guiding presence in my life. In Jesus' name, we pray. **Amen.**

VI. Praise

"Through the LORD's mercies we are not consumed, Because His compassions fail not. They are new every morning; Great is Your faithfulness. "The LORD is my portion," says my soul, "Therefore I hope in Him!"

Lamentations 3:22-24 NKJV

Merciful Father, thank you for new mercies, for your compassion, for your love. Thank you for your grace that does not allow our sorrows to consume us. Thank you for being with me, Lord; therefore, I have hope in You. Glorious, Lord. Thank you. In Jesus' name, we pray. **Amen.**

VII. *Praise*

"O Lord, You are my God. I will exalt You, I will praise Your name, For You have done wonderful things; Your counsels of old are faithfulness and truth."

Isaiah 25:1 NKJV

Marvelous God of the ages. Thank you for all that you have done and will do in my life.Thank you for teaching me that your promises are faithful, true, and will come to pass. Father, I praise you in advance for these thy gifts - yesterday, today, and tomorrow. In Jesus' name, we pray. **Amen.**

Prayers for the Journey

The Benediction

The Benediction

"Now may the God of hope fill you with all joy and peace in believing, that you may abound in hope by the power of the Holy Spirit."

Romans 15:13 NKJV

Scripture Index

Guidance

Strength

Comfort

Praise

About The Author

Vernet Clemons Nettles, EdD is a parent, educator, speaker, and writing coach. Throughout the years, she has served in various capacities of church service. Professionally, Dr. Nettles has worked in public education for more than 30 years.

Dr. Nettles believes that God has not promised daily sunshine and rainbows; however, He has promised glorious days of his grace, mercy, and loving presence. It is my desire that these prayers inspire you in good or bad times.

Let's stay connected:

www.vernetcnettles.com

www.vcndailypray.com

vernetcnettles@gmail.com

Made in the USA
Columbia, SC
06 October 2024

43163191R00042